Mental Magic

Surefire Tricks to Amaze Your Friends

Martin Gardner
Illustrated by Jeff Sinclair

Sterling Publishing Co., Inc.
New York

Edited by Claire Bazinet

Library of Congress Cataloging-in-Publication Data
Gardner, Martin, 1914–
    Mental magic:surefire tricks to amaze your friends / by Martin
Gardner; illustrated by Jeff Sinclair.
        p.   cm.
    Includes index.
    Summary: A collection of math tricks using the magic of num-
bers in which the marvelous Professor Picanumba can seemingly
predict random events in dozens of numerical exercises. Includes
answers at the end.
    ISBN 0-8069-2049-1
    1. Mathematical recreations Juvenile literature. [1. Mathematical
recreations. 2. Magic tricks.] I. Sinclair, Jeff. illus. II. Title.
    QA95.G2917   1999
    793.7'4—dc21   99-37658
                                                                      CIP
10 9 8 7 6 5 4 3 2 1

Published by Sterling Publishing Company, Inc.
387 Park Avenue South, New York, N.Y. 10016
© 1999 by Martin Gardner
Distributed in Canada by Sterling Publishing
℅ Canadian Manda Group, One Atlantic Avenue, Suite 105
Toronto, Ontario, Canada M6K 3E7
Distributed in Great Britain and Europe by Chris Lloyd
463 Ashley Road, Parkstone, Poole, Dorset, BH14 0AX, England
Distributed in Australia by Capricorn Link (Australia) Pty Ltd.
P.O. Box 6651, Baulkham Hills, Business Centre, NSW 2153, Australia
Manufactured in the United States of America
All rights reserved

Sterling ISBN 0-8069-2049-1

Dedication

To my sweet, adorable, brilliant,
wonderful, long-suffering wife...
who wrote this dedication

Acknowledgments

Many friends and correspondents, most of them amateur magicians, invented items for this book. I list them here alphabetically:

Tom Batchelor, Paul Curry, Karl Fulves, Shigeo Futigawa, Bob Hummer, Max Maven, Tony Miller, Mitsunabu Matsuyama, Charles Reynolds, George Sands, Joseph Schmidt, and Jim Steinmeyer.

There are others who may have devised some of the tricks without my knowing. Many of the exercises are my own ideas.

I also thank my wife Charlotte for her usual skill in copyediting and proofing galleys.

Foreword

Professor Picanumba, who for many years lived alone in a cave near the top of a distant high mountain, has developed the incredible ability to predict what you will do. Here in this book, our esteemed professor presents a series of tests in which you are asked to freely select certain numbers, words, or pictures. In the back of the book, the professor, having accessed his great power of precognition, has had printed there the outcome of each exercise—before you've even done it!

Work your way carefully through each test, doing just what the professor has asked you to do. When you arrive at the final outcome, turn to the page at the back of the book, in the section headed "Professor Picanumba Predicts," for his prediction under the name of the exercise. You'll be amazed by how accurate the old fellow is!

Almost every time, the professor will predict exactly the final result of each test. On a couple of occasions he has made a guess that may or may not be correct, but most of the time his guesses will be right on the mark.

Before starting these tests, you should have on hand a deck of cards, four dice, a calculator, a pencil and a supply of paper. A few puzzles require using other items, but they are usually available around the home.

The word "digit," used throughout the book, means one of the numerals 0, 1, 2, 3, 4, 5, 6, 7, 8 and 9.

Martin Gardner, D.F.
(Doctor of Flimflam)

Contents

The Tests

Wonderland Spell

Here is how Lewis Carroll began *Alice in Wonderland*:

> Alice was beginning to get very tired of sitting by her sister on the bank, and of having nothing to do: once or twice she had peeped into the book her sister was reading.

Select any of the first 12 words. Starting on the next word, spell the word you chose, tapping a word for each letter. For example, 1f you selected the word "Alice" you spell A-L-I-C-E. Counting words for letters, this takes you to the word "very." So you spell V-E-R-Y, next ending on "by." Keep going. Note the word on which your spelling chain ends. What's the word?

Answer on page 90.

A Mysterious Matrix

Make a copy of the 6-by-6 matrix on the page opposite.

Circle any number, then cross out all the numbers in the same row and the same column as the number you circled.

Select any number *not* crossed out and circle it. Again, cross out all numbers in the same row and same column as the circled number.

Repeat this four more times. There will be six circled numbers, each randomly chosen.

Add the six numbers. What's the total?

Answer on page 84.

28	26	30	27	29	25
34	32	36	33	35	31
16	14	18	15	17	13
4	2	6	3	5	1
10	8	12	9	11	7
22	20	24	21	23	19

Cards that Shake Dice

In this exercise you use a deck of cards to simulate the tossing of a pair of dice.

Shuffle the cards, then start dealing them face up to form pile A. Stop as soon as a card turns up with a value of 1 through 6. This number represents the toss of one die.

As soon as you get a die number on pile A, start dealing a new pile B. Again, stop as soon as a card appears with a value of 1 through 6. This represents the toss of another die. Add the two numbers, and write the sum on a sheet of paper. The sum is as randomly obtained as if you had tossed a pair of dice.

After recording the results of the first "throw" of imaginary dice, shove the two piles aside and repeat the dealing into two more piles, to obtain a second dice "throw." Write the results of this second "throw" below the previous number.

Continue making "throws" in this manner until the entire deck has been used. Add all the "throws." Because each "throw" was as random as a toss of two dice, it seems impossible that Professor Picanumba could predict the sum of all the "throws."

What's the final sum?

Answer on page 81.

Try This on a Dollar Bill

Write down the number on any dollar bill. Scramble the digits any way you like—that is, mix up their order. Jot down this second number.

Using your calculator, subtract the smaller number from the larger.

From the difference, take 7.

Copy the digits now on display, then add them all together. If the sum is more than one digit, add the digits once more. Keep adding the digits in the sums until just one digit is obtained.

What is it?

Answer on page 89.

The Magic of 8

Multiply your phone number (disregard its area code) by 8. Write down the following three numbers:

1. Your phone number.

2. 8.

3. The product of your phone number and 8.

Add all the digits in those three numbers. If the sum is more than one digit, add again. Continue in this way until a single digit is reached.

What's the digit?

Answer on page 84.

Around the Square

Toss a die on the table. Enter the number it shows into your calculator.

Multiply the number by 8.

Add 4.

Add the number on top of the die.

Now, on the grid below, put your finger on cell A and say "One." Tap clockwise around the square, tapping the cells as you go, and counting, 2, 3, 4, and so on. Stop tapping when you reach the number in your calculator's display.

On what letter did your finger end the count?

Answer on page 80.

Nation, Animals, Fruit

Write down the following words:

1. The name of a nation that begins with D.

2. An animal that begins with the second letter of the nation.

3. The color of the animal.

4. An animal that begins with the *last* letter of the nation.

5. A fruit that begins with the last letter of the animal selected in step 4.

As a bonus, Professor Picanumba will tell you where you got those shoes you are wearing.

Answers on page 85.

The Red and the Black

Shuffle a deck of cards, then deal 30 cards to the table to form a pile.

Count the number of black cards in the pile. From this number subtract the number of red cards in the rest of the deck. What's the difference?

Here's a quick question. If you add up all the digits in 1234567890 the sum is 45. If instead you multiply all the digits, will the product be more or less than 100?

Answers on page 86.

The Exact Word

Think of any word on this page. Concentrate on it, then turn to the answer section. Believe it or not, the answer will print the exact word!

Answer on page 82.

A Two-Dice Test

Toss a die. Think of a number from 1 through 6. Put another die on top of the one you tossed, turning it so the number you thought of is on top of the stack.

Carefully check the numbers on the two faces of the dice that are touching. Add those two numbers to the number you thought of, and write it down.

Think of another number from 1 through 6. Add it to the last result.

Remove the top die of the stack. Turn it so your second selected number is on top. Remove it from the stack and place it alongside the other die.

Lift up both dice. Add the sum of their *bottom* faces to your previous total.

What's your final sum?

Answer on page 89.

A Curious Count

Shuffle a deck of cards, then start dealing them face up to form a pile. Say "Ten" when you deal the first card, "Nine" when you deal the second, "Eight" when you deal the third, and so on. In other words, as you deal you count backward from 10 to 1.

Assume that each face card (king, queen, or jack) has a value of 10.

As soon as you deal a card with a value that is the same as the number you say aloud, stop dealing and start a new pile. If you reach 10 without finding a match, "kill" the pile by putting a card face down on top of it.

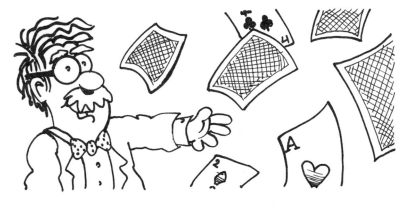

Repeat this procedure until you have dealt four piles. If all four have been "killed," which is very unlikely, start the test all over again after another shuffle of the deck.

After the four piles are finished, add the values of the cards at the top of each "living" pile. Call this sum "k".

Deal "k" cards from the remainder of the deck, then count the cards that remain.

How many are they?

Answer on page 81.

A Rotating Matrix

Think a number from 1 through 16. Locate that number on the border of the matrix below. Turn the page so the number is at the top of the matrix.

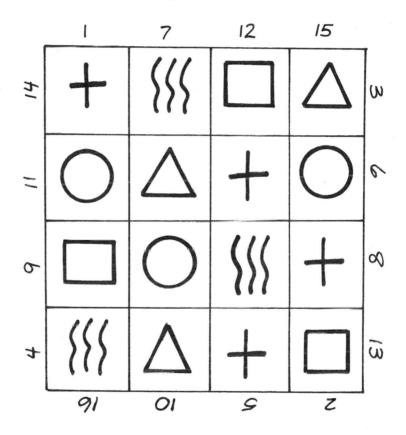

Count the cells from left to right, top to bottom, starting the count on the top left corner cell. Note the symbol in the cell where the count ends.

What symbol is it?

Answer on page 86.

Catch the Bill

Hold a dollar bill by one end as shown. Position your right hand so your thumb is on one side, fingers on the other, as if you were about to catch the bill when your left hand drops it. Your thumb and fingers must not touch the bill.

Let go of the bill with your left hand, and you will find that it is very easy to catch it in the other hand before the bill falls to the floor.

Now let someone else hold the bill while you try to catch it after it is dropped.

Can you catch the bill before it falls?

Answer on page 81.

Five in a Row

Remove from a deck the nine of diamonds, the four of hearts, the queen of hearts, the ace of diamonds, and the seven of clubs.

Place the five cards face up in a row in the order shown here.

As you can see, there is one picture card, one ace, and one black card. Look them over carefully. Select one of the five cards and write it down.

Your choice is entirely free. What card did you write down?

Answer on page 82.

Reverse, Subtract, Add

Write down any three-digit number provided no zero is used and that the first and last digits differ by more than 1.

Reverse the three digits to make a second number. For example, if you thought of 387 the reverse number would be 783.

Subtract the smaller number of the two from the larger. Reverse the result, then add it to the previous number.

Now translate the sum into a word by using the following chart:

S	M	A	R	T
1	2	3	4	5
6	7	8	9	0

For each digit in the sum, substitute the letter at the top of the chart. What word do you get?

Answer on page 86.

20

A Geometry Test

Draw a simple geometrical figure. Inside it draw another simple geometric figure.
  What did you draw?

Answer on page 83.

Monkey Business

If you had ten bananas and a monkey stole all but six how many bananas would you have left?

Answer on page 84

Face-Up Cards

Divide a deck into two halves of 26 cards each. Turn one half over so all its cards are face up. Shuffle them into the other half, which remains face down. Keep shuffling as long as you like, until you are satisfied the cards are thoroughly mixed.

Deal 26 cards to the table to form a pile. Put the rest of the deck down to make a second pile. Turn over either pile.

Count the number of face-up cards in each pile.

What is the difference between the two counts?

Answer on page 82

What's on the Paper?

Write any word you like on a sheet of paper. Fold the paper twice, then put it down and stand on it. Believe it or not, Professor Picanumba will tell you what is on the paper!

In addition, the professor will explain a method that enables you to see right through the walls of a house!

Answers on page 89.

Count the Clips

Remove the contents of a small box of paper clips. Place exactly 20 clips in the box and set the rest of them aside.

Select a number fewer than ten. Take that number of clips out of the box and put them in your pocket.

Count the number of clips remaining in the box. Add the two digits of the count and remove that number of paper clips from the box. Put them in your pocket.

Take out three more paper clips.

How many clips are left in the box?

Answer on page 81.

Number, Flower, Color

Think of a number between 10 and 50 that consists of two different digits, both of them odd. The numbers 11 and 33 are ruled out because their digits are alike. Write down the number you selected.

Under the number write the name of a flower.

Under the flower write a color. Most people think first of red, so *don't* pick red.

What are your three choices?

Answers on page 85.

In Praise of Red

Red is the color of sunsets and fire,
And red is our blood when it flows.

A beautiful red are the lips of my love.
They rival the red of a rose.

We thrill to the red of a cardinal's wings,
But not to a sunburned red nose!

* * *

Roll one of your dice on the table.
Let "n" be the number it shows.

Look at the "n"th line of the poem above. Count to the "n"th word of that "n"th line.

What is the word?

Answer on page 83.

24

Three Heaps

Form three heaps of paper clips in a row on the table. Each heap must contain the same number of clips and there must be more than three clips in each heap. (If paper clips are not handy, you can use beans, raisins, match sticks, toothpicks, or any other set of small objects.)

Take three clips from each end heap and put them on the middle heap. Count the number of clips in either end heap. Remove that number of clips from the center heap and place them on one of the end heaps.

Take a single clip from either end heap and put it in the middle heap.

How many clips are now in the middle heap?

Answer on page 88.

Fold and Trim

Fold a sheet of paper in half four times, then unfold it. The creases will form a 4-by-4 matrix of cells as shown below.

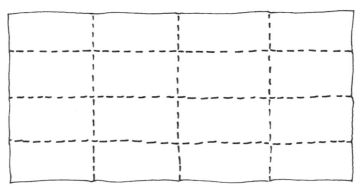

Number the cells from 1 through 16 as shown on the page opposite. Fold each crease forward and back a few times so the paper will fold easily either way along each crease.

Now fold the sheet into a packet the size of one cell. You can make the folds as tricky as you please, folding this way, that way—any way you like. You may even tuck folds between folds. In other words, make the folding as random as possible until you have a packet the size of a single cell.

With the scissors trim away all four edges of the folded paper packet so that it consists of sixteen separate pieces. Spread the pieces on the table. Some pieces will have their number-side up, others their number-side down.

Add all the numbers on the face-up pieces. What is the sum?

Answer on page 82.

Number Names

Think of any number from 1 through 100. Write down its name.

  Count the number of letters in its name to obtain a second number.

  Count the number of letters in the second number to obtain a third number.

  Continue in this way until the chain of numbers ends on a number that keeps repeating.

  What is this number?

Answer on page 85.

A Test with Two Dice

Roll a pair of dice on the table. Call them A and B. Write down the following four different products:

1. The product of the top numbers on the dice.

2. The product of their bottom numbers.

3. The product of the top of A and the bottom of B.

4. The product of the top of B and the bottom of A.

  Add the four products.
  What is the sum?

Answer on page 88.

Think-a-Letter

Select any one of the twenty-six letters of the alphabet. Look for your thought-of letter in each of the five columns below. Write down the letter at the top of each column in which your selected letter appears.

Change these letters to numbers, using the code A = 1, B = 2, C = 3, D = 4, and so on. Add the numbers that you obtain in this way.

Using the same code, turn the sum you get back into a letter. What letter does it yield?

A	B	D	H	P
C	C	E	I	Q
E	F	F	J	R
G	G	G	K	S
I	J	L	L	T
K	K	M	M	U
M	N	N	N	V
O	O	O	O	W
Q	R	T	X	X
S	S	U	Y	Y
U	V	V	Z	Z
W	W	W		
Y	Z			

Answer on page 88.

Turn Two and Cut

Hold a packet of ten cards face down in your left hand. Turn the top pair of cards face up, then cut the packet at any spot you like. Again, turn the top two cards face up and cut. Keep up this turning a pair and cutting for as long as you like. This, of course, will randomize the positions of the face-up cards in the packet.

After you decide to stop reversing and cutting, deal the cards in a row on the table. Reverse all the cards at even positions along the row; that is, turn over the second, fourth, sixth, eighth, and tenth card.

How many cards in the row will now be face up?

Answer on page 89.

The Rotated Die

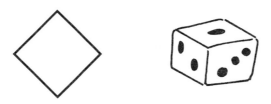

Place a die on the square shape above so that you can see it's 1, 2, 3 faces, as shown on the right.

Give the die a quarter turn in any of two ways. You may rotate it clockwise or the other way, keeping it on the square, or you can tip it over an edge in any of the four directions, then slide it back onto the square. Each turn replaces one of the three visible faces by another face.

After you have made 13 random turns, add the three faces you now see. Is the sum odd or even.?

Answer on page 86.

An ABCABC Number

Think of any three-digit number ABC. Enter it twice into your calculator as a six-digit number ABCABC.

Seven and 11 are lucky dice numbers, and 13 is considered an unlucky number.

Divide ABCABC by 7. Professor Picanumba predicts there will be no remainder. Sure enough, he's right!

Divide the result now on display by 11. The Professor again predicts correctly that there is no remainder.

Finally, divide the number on display by 13. Once more, there is no remainder.

What number is now showing on your calculator?

Answer on page 80.

A Domino Chain

You need a complete set of 28 dominoes to do this test. Remove the one domino that has spots 2 and 5. Put it in your pocket.

Now pretend that you are playing a solitaire game of dominoes. Form the 27 pieces into one long single chain, placing them any way you like. When completed, note the number of spots at each end of the chain.

What are those two numbers?

Answer on page 81.

The GRY Test

Think of a word that ends in GRY.

Professor Picanumba will tell you the word that you thought of. As a bonus, he'll tell you within four days the day you were born!

Now, how about a little riddle? A cowboy rode into Bottleneck on Friday, stayed three days, then rode out of town on Friday. How come?

Answers on page 83.

Whisk the Dime

Hold your left hand palm up and put a dime on the center of the palm.

With a whisk broom in your other hand, try to brush the dime off your left hand.

Can you do it?

Here's another riddle. A barber in Chicago says he'd rather cut the hair of ten red-headed men than the hair of one brown-haired man. Can you guess why?

Answers on page 90.

Beast, City, Vegetable

Write down words for the following:

1. A wild beast.

2. The largest city of a foreign country.

3. A vegetable.

What are the three words?

Answers on page 80.

A Test with Your Age

Enter your age in the calculator.
  Multiply it by 12.
  Add the mysterious number 2856.
  Divide by 3.
  Divide by 4.
  Subtract your age.
  What number is now on display?

Answer on page 88.

A Surprising Sum

On the opposite page are four circles. Copy them on a sheet of paper.

Choose any number in Circle 1. Cross it out, then write it down as the first digit of a number that you are creating.

Select any digit in Circle 2. Cross it out. Put it down as the second digit of the number you are forming.

Select a digit in Circle 3. Cross it out and make it the third digit of your number.

Select a digit in Circle 4. Cross it out. This will be the fourth and last digit of your number.

Now create three more four-digit numbers in exactly the same way. Select the digits from the four circles, taking the circles in 1, 2, 3, 4 order. Cross out digits as you use them.

You now have randomly formed four numbers, each with four digits. Add the four random numbers.

What's the total?

Answer on page 87.

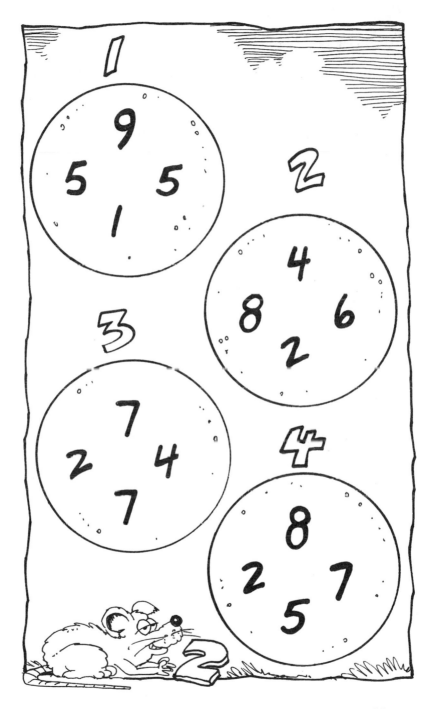

35

Around the Solar System

For this test you need a dime and eight pennies.

Place a dime on any of the nine cells shown on the opposite page.

Spell the name on that cell by moving the dime one step in any direction—up, down, left, or right—to an adjacent square. Diagonal moves are not permitted. At each move spell a letter. For example, if you put the dime on Mars, spell M-A-R-S by moving the dime in any of the possible directions, one move for each letter. You can imagine that the dime is a spaceship moving around the solar system.

After you have moved the dime by spelling, put a penny on Venus. From now on you must not move the dime to a cell occupied by a penny.

Move the dime seven times, then put a penny on Mars.
Move three times. Put a penny on Mercury.
Move seven times. Put a penny on Uranus.
Move five times. Put a penny on Neptune.
Move nine times. Put a penny on Saturn.
Move three times. Put a penny on Jupiter.
Move once. Put a penny on the Moon.

Where, now, is the dime?

Answer on page 80.

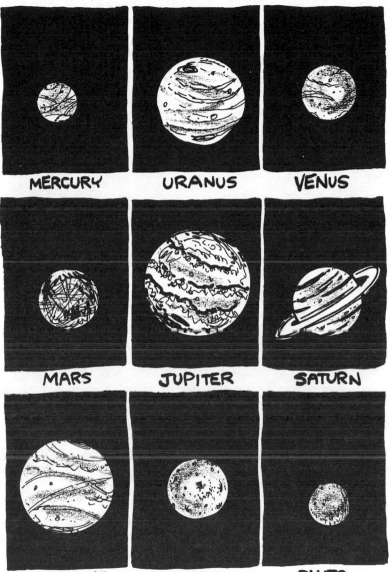

Think-a-Digit

Choose a digit from 1 through 9. Enter it three times in your calculator. For example, if you picked 8, enter 888.

Divide this number by 3.

Divide the result by the number you thought of.

What number is now on display?

Answer on page 88.

A Remarkable Number

Enter 999999 in your calculator, then divide it by seven. The result will be a mysterious number.

Multiply this number by any number obtained by tossing a die.

Arrange the digits of the product in increasing order, starting with the smallest digit, then the next higher one, and so on to the largest digit. This will form a six-digit number.

What is the number?

Answer on page 86.

Heads or Tails?

You need seven pennies for this test. Spin them one at a time on a hard surface. Or, if you prefer, carefully balance all seven pennies on their edge, then bang the table to make them all fall over.

After all seven coins have fallen flat, will there be more heads showing than tails, or vice versa?

Answer on page 83.

Drop the Coin

Put your two hands together like this.

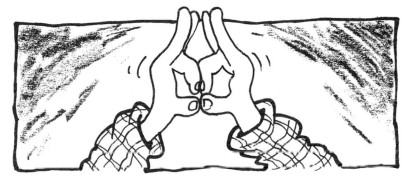

Ask someone to put a coin between the tips of your third fingers.

If you keep your middle fingers pressed firmly together as shown, you'll find it easy to separate the tips of your thumbs, index fingers, and pinkies.

Can you move the tips of your third fingers apart to let the coin fall?

Answer on page 81.

At the Apex

Copy the triangle of circles on the facing page.

Put any four digits you like in the four vacant circles of the bottom row. They needn't be all different, and you may include one or more zeros if you like.

The remaining circles are filled with digits as follows:

Add two adjacent pairs of numbers, divide the sum by 5, and put the remainder in the circle just above the adjacent pair of numbers.

For example, suppose two adjacent numbers in the bottom row are 6 and 8. They add to 14. Dividing 14 by 5 gives a remainder of 4, so you put 4 directly above the 6 and 8. If there is no remainder (such as 6 + 4 = 10) then put a zero above the 6 and 4.

Continue in this way, going up the triangle, until all the circles have digits.

What digit is at the apex of the triangle?

Answer on page 80.

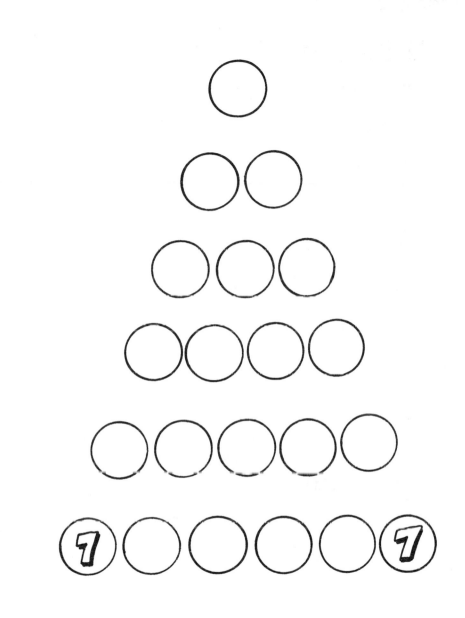

A Calculator Test

Think of any digit from 1 through 9. Enter it in your calculator.

Multiply it by 11.

Divide the result by the sum of its digits.

What do you get on the display?

Answer on page 81.

A Peculiar Series

Think of a number. It can be of any size. Jot it down.

Add 7 to the number and put the sum down to the right of the chosen number.

Add 7 again to get a third number.

Add 7 once more to get a fourth number. You now have a row of four numbers.

Multiply the two end numbers and write down the product.

Multiply the two middle numbers and write down the product.

Subtract the smaller product from the larger.

What is the result?

Answer on page 85.

Rotating Spoon

Hold the end of a spoon by the handle, with the bowl of the spoon upside down. Flip the spoon in the air so it makes a complete somersault, and catch it by the end.

It's a good idea to do this over a bed to avoid the clatter, because you may drop the spoon many times before you succeed in catching it.

When you do catch the handle, will the spoon's bowl be right side up or upside down?

Answer on page 86.

Another Calculator Test

Your calculator keyboard has a square of digits from 1 through 9. Select any row, column, or main diagonal.

Arrange the three digits you selected in any order, then jot them down on paper as a three-digit number. For example, if you selected the middle column, you have the digits 852. You can put them in any order you like, such as 528, 285, and so on.

Select another row, column, or main diagonal. Do the same thing with its three digits to make a second three-digit number. Write it down.

Using the calculator, multiply one of the three-digit numbers by the other.

Add all the digits in the product. Call the sum "k".

Turn to the magic circle of symbols on the opposite page. Put your finger on the star, calling it 1, then tap your finger clockwise around the circle, counting, 2, 3, 4,....until you reach the number "k".

What symbol did your count stop on?

Answer on page 80.

Four Queens

Put the four queens on top of the deck, then add eight indifferent cards on top of the queens.

Think of a number from 10 through 19. Deal that many cards from the deck to the table. Add the two digits in the number you selected. Call the sum "k".

Transfer "k" cards from the table back to the top of the deck. Remove the top card of the pile on the table. Without looking at its face, place it aside.

Put the pile back on the deck. Think of another number from 10 through 19, and repeat the procedure just described. Do it two more times, with two other freely chosen numbers.

You now have four face-down cards on the table. Turn them over. What are they?

Answer on page 83.

A Four-Dice Test

Place four dice on the table and arrange them so all four top numbers are the same.

Turn two dice upside down and add the top numbers. What's the sum?

Answer on page 82.

A Test with 66

Write down any number from 50 through 100.
  Add 66.
  Note the last two digits of the sum. Call this number
"k".
  Subtract "k" from the number you first thought of.
  What's the result?

  Just for good measure, do you know why no one played
cards on Noah's Ark?

Answers on page 87.

246,913,578

Enter the above "strange" number, the title of this test,
into your calculator. Now, you may freely choose to do
any of the following:
  Multiply the number by 2, 4, 5, 7, 8, 10, 11, 13, 16,
20, 22, 25, 26, 31, 35, 40, 55, 65, 125, 175, or 875!
  Or, if you prefer, divide the number by 2, 4, 5, or 8!
  After you have done one of the above multiplications
or divisions, rearrange the digits of the result in serial
order from the smallest digit to the largest. Ignore any
zeros among the digits.
  The result will be a number of nine digits. What is this
number?

Answer on page 89.

Funny Fractions

Consider the following compound fraction:

$$\frac{a/b}{c/d}$$

Rearrange the terms to form another compound fraction:

For the terms a, b, c, and d, substitute any digits you like.

Determine the difference between the two compound fractions.

What is it?

$$\frac{d/c}{b/a}$$

Answer on page 83.

Topsy Turvy Fun

For a change of pace, Professor Picanumba says to try the following stunts on your calculator. After doing the specified multiplications or divisions, turn your calculator around to read its display upside down.

1. Say "Hi!", then divide 6.1872 by 8.

2. What do friends say after you fool them with a magic trick? Divide 31563 by 7.

3. What did Santa Claus say when Rudolph showed him one of these stunts? Multiply .06734 by 6.

4. What's the capital of Idaho? Multiply 8777 by 4.

Answers on page 88.

A Trick With Three Dice

Toss three dice on the table. Call them A, B, and C.

Write down the total showing on A and B.

Turn B and C upside down and write the total showing.

Turn upside down C and A and write the total.

Add the three sums.

What's the result?

Answer on page 89.

Four Kings

Put the four kings on top of the deck, then cut the deck into four approximately equal piles. The piles should be in a row in front of you, with the pile that was formerly the deck's top on the right end of the row.

Pick up the leftmost pile. Deal three cards into the spot where it stood, then deal a single card on top of each of the other three piles. Replace the rest of the pile on top of the three cards you just dealt to the spot where the pile was before.

Repeat this same procedure with each of the other three piles.

Turn over the top card of each pile.

What cards are they?

Answer on page 83.

Pairing Cards

Deal 28 cards to the table, turn them face up, then shuffle them into the rest of the deck. Shuffle a few more times to make sure the deck is a random mixture of face-down and face-up cards.

From the top of the deck remove a pair of cards. If one is face up and the other face down, toss the pair aside.

If both cards are face up, put them at the left of the table. If both are face down, put them at the right.

Continue taking cards from the top of the deck in pairs. If the pair is a mixture—one card up, the other down—toss it aside. If both cards are alike, place them left or right as explained.

After you have gone through the entire deck, you will have a pile of face-up cards on the left, and a pile of face-down cards on the right. Count the number of cards in each pile. Subtract the smaller number from the larger.

What's the difference?

Answer on page 85.

Where's the Dime?

Place a dime or small coin on any of the white squares in the matrix on the opposite page, then make the following moves:

1. Move the dime left or right to the nearest gray square.

2. Move the dime up or down to the nearest white square.

3. Move the dime diagonally to the nearest gray square.

4. Move the dime either down or to the right to the nearest white square.

On what square is the dime now resting?

Answer on page 90.

What's the Word?

Crease a sheet of paper as shown below and letter the eight cells from A to H.

Fold the sheet into a packet eight leaves deep by folding it any way you like along the creases. After you do this, some cells in the packet will face one way, other cells will face the opposite way. Because you made the folds at random, there seems to be no way to know which cells face which way.

Trim the four sides of the packet with scissors, so that no cell is attached to another cell.

Spread the pieces on the table. Can you arrange the face-up pieces to spell a common English word? If you can, stop. If you can't, turn over all the pieces.

Try again to spell a word with the face-up pieces.

You are sure to succeed. What word do you spell?

Answer on page 90.

Three Surprises

Enter 777 in your calculator. Multiply it by your age.

1. Multiply the result by 13. Are you surprised?

2. Now, try this: Enter 1443. Multiply it by your age, then by 7.

3. For a third surprise, enter 3367. Multiply by your age, then by 3.

Answers on page 88.

Another Calculator Surprise

Enter 987654312 in your calculator. Note that the last two numbers, 1 and 2, are interchanged.
  Divide by 8. What's the surprise?

As a bonus, Professor Picanumba will tell you how you can throw a ball so it stops in midair, reverses direction, and comes back to you!

Answers on page 80.

A Surprising Fraction

Write down to be added a series of odd-only numbers in serial order starting with 1:

$$1 + 3 + 5 + 7 + 9 + 11 + ...$$

Continue the series for as many numerical terms as you like, provided the number of terms is even.

Let the first half of the series be the numerator of a fraction, and the second half of the series be the fraction's denominator; for example, if you stopped after six terms the fraction would be:

$$\frac{1 + 3 + 5}{7 + 9 + 11}$$

Add the number of terms above the line, then add the series of terms below the line. Then reduce the fraction you get to its lowest terms.

What fraction do you end up with?

Answer on page 87.

Where's the Ace?

Find the ace of spades and place it face up on top of the deck.

Think of a number from 10 through 19. Call it "k."

Deal "k" cards to the table. The bottom of the pile you dealt will, of course, be the *reversed* ace of spades. Place this pile on top of the deck.

Add the two digits of "k", then transfer that many cards from the top of the deck to the bottom.

How far down in the deck is the ace of spades?

Answer on page 90.

A Letter in Washington

Multiply together all eight digits in the number on a dollar bill. Add all the digits in the product. The sum will have two digits.

Add the two digits. If the result is another 2-digit number, add again. Keep adding until a single digit remains.

Call this digit "k".

Count to the "k"th letter in **WASHINGTON**.

What's the letter?

Answer on page 84.

Four File Cards

Write 39 on one side of a file card, and 51 on the other side. On a second file card write 26 and 34 on the two sides. A third card gets 65 and 85. A fourth card gets 52 and 68.

Place the four cards on the table so the numbers showing on top are 26, 39, 52, and 65.

Slide any card out of the row, then turn over the three remaining cards. Slide out another card, and turn over the remaining two cards.

Slide out a third card. Turn over the card that remains.

You now have a choice of leaving the cards as they are, or turning all of them over.

With your calculator, multiply all the numbers showing. What's the product?

Answer on page 82.

The Missing 8

Enter 12345679 in your calculator. Note that the 8 is missing from the series.

Multiply the series by 3.

Multiply the result by any digit from 1 through 9.

Multiply once more by 3.

What's the surprising result?

Answer on page 84.

An 8-Card Test

Place the six of spades and the ten of hearts back to back and fasten them together with a paper clip.

Do the same thing with the following pairs:

Seven of spades and jack of hearts.
Eight of spades and queen of hearts.
Nine of spades and king of hearts.

Put these four "double-face cards" in a row on the table, hearts side up on all cards. Or, if you prefer, the four may have their spade sides uppermost.

Select any two of the double-face cards and turn them over. Add the values of the cards on top. The jack has a value of 11, the queen 12, and the king 13.

What's the sum?

Answer on page 82.

An Unexpected Number

This is not a prediction test, but merely a test of your ability to recognize a famous number.

Start with 1234. Switch 1 and 2, and switch 3 and 4, to get 2143. Enter it in your calculator.

Divide by 22, then hit the square root key twice.

What do you get?

Answer on page 89.

Five Coins

Place on the table in a row, in order from left to right, a penny, dime, nickel, half dollar, and a quarter. (If you don't have a half dollar handy, write "50¢" on a small piece of paper and use it instead of the coin.

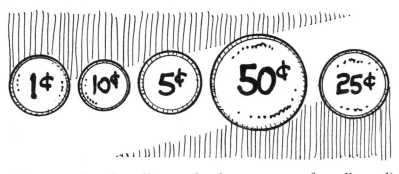

Put a marker (small toy, checker, square of cardboard) on any of the five coins. Move it back and forth, from coin to adjacent coin, as many times as indicated by the value of cents in the coin on which you placed it. For example, if you put the marker on the quarter, your first move must be left, but after that you can move it either left or right as you count the moves to 25. If the folder is on the penny, you move it only once, and so on for the other coins.

After you have moved the marker the required number of times, Professor Picanumba says the penny will be uncovered. Take away the penny.

Again move the folder a number of times indicated by the coin on which it now rests. The Professor says this will leave the quarter uncovered. Take it away.

Three coins remain. Move the marker once.

On what coin is the folder?

Answer on page 82.

The Stubborn Rubber Band

Attach a rubber band to your fingers as shown below.

Without using your other hand, or without rubbing the band against anything, can you get the band off your hand?

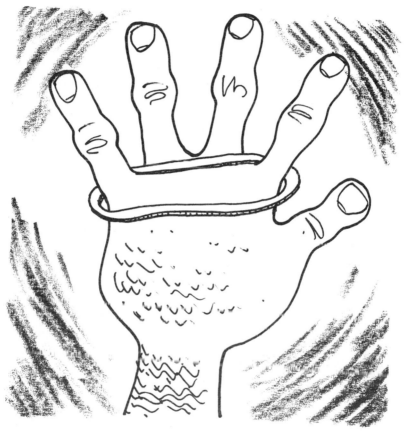

While you are working with the rubber band, here's something for your brain. If you divide the number of your toes by 1/2, then multiply the result by the number of your fingers, what do you get?

Answer on page 87.

The Rotating Tubes

Place two paper towel or toilet tissue tubes side by side and balance a yardstick on top.

If you rotate the tubes inward, as shown by the arrows, the yardstick will remain balanced on the tubes. It may shift slightly back and forth, but it stays balanced.

Test it out and see for yourself.

Now, testing your own mental magic, what do you suppose would happen if you tried rotating the two tubes the opposite way; that is, away from each other?

Answer on page 86.

A Three-Dice Stack

You need three dice for this test. Toss the first die on the table. Toss a second die, pick it up in your fingers and place it right on top of the first die. The third die goes on top of the other two, turned so its top face is 1.

If you inspect this stack from all sides, you'll note that five faces cannot be seen. Add these faces as follows:

Check the two touching faces between the top and middle dice. Write down their sum, and put the top die aside.

Check the two hidden faces that are touching between the two dice that remain. Add the numbers, write down the sum, and put the top die aside.

Check the bottom face of the remaining die. Write it down. Add the three numbers you have written.

What's their sum?

Answer on page 88.

One, Two, Three

Choose a single digit from the numbers one, two, and three.

Multiply it by the digit eight.
Subtract three.
To the result add the digit you first selected.
Call the sum "k".
Count to the "k"th word of these instructions.
What word is it?

Answer on page 85

Test of Finger Strength

Hold a toothpick between the ends of your fingers as we show you below.

Can you break the pick by pressing down with the tips of your index and third finger?

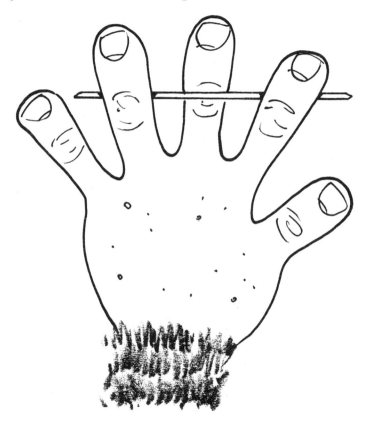

While you are trying to break the toothpick, Professor Pincanumber wants you to ponder this: The capital of Kentucky is not pronounced Looey-ville or Lewis-ville. What's the correct pronunciation?

Answers on page 87.

A 3 by 4 Test

Make a copy of this 3 by 4 matrix.

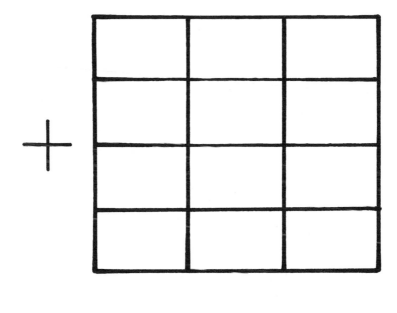

Put digits 1 through 9 in the cells in any way you like. Three empty cells will remain. In those cells put either three ones, or three fours, or three sevens.

Treat each row of the matrix as a 3-digit number. Add these four numbers by writing the sum over the four lines below the matrix.

Add the sum's four digits. If the result is more than one digit, add those two numbers. Keep adding until only one digit remains.

What is this digit?

Answer on page 88.

The Curious Q

Think of a number between 10 and 50 inclusive.

Put your finger on the bottom symbol in the tail of the Q on the facing page. Say "One." Tap the next symbol above it and say "Two." Continue upward, counting at each tap, until you reach the star, then turn right and continue tapping *counterclockwise* around the circle until you say the number you originally thought of. The tapping may take you more than once around the circle. If it does, ignore the tail of the Q as you go around.

After you tap the symbol at the count of your chosen number, pause and reverse direction. You now tap *clockwise* around the circle, ignoring the tail. Say "One" for the symbol you last tapped. Don't make the mistake of starting your count on the symbol next to it. When you reach the number you first selected, note the symbol where the count ends.

What symbol is it?

Answer on page 81.

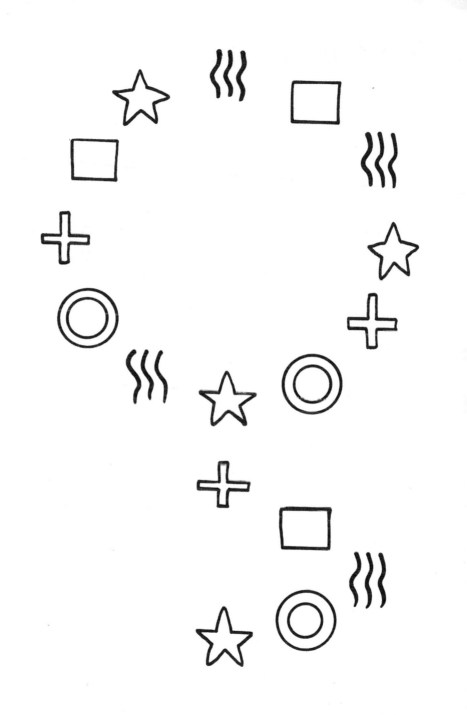

The Four Knights

Place a penny on each of the four central squares on the checkerboard shown on the opposite page.

The pennies move like the knight piece in chess —that is, two squares up, down, left, or right (not diagonally), then one square at right angles to the previous move.

Select any of the "knights" and move it as many times as indicated by the number on its starting square. Write down the color (black or white), of the cell where it landed. Remove the penny. It is okay for a penny to land on top of another penny.

Repeat this with another penny. After it has moved according to the number on its starting square, again write down the color of the square where it stopped, and take away the penny.

Repeat this procedure with the other two pennies.

What are the four colors you have listed?

Answer on page 83.

Around the Circle

Jot down the last two digits of your phone number. Add them, then subtract this sum from the original 2-digit number. Call the difference "k."

Put a finger on the cross at the top of the circle of symbols on the opposite page. Say "One." Now tap the symbols clockwise around the circle, counting as you go, until you tap the symbol corresponding to "k".

On what symbol does this count end?

Answer on page 80.

Deal and Switch

Arrange the spade cards of a deck in order from ace to king, with the ace on top of a packet of thirteen face-down cards.

As you deal these cards to form a face-down pile, mix their order as follows:

Either deal a single card, or take a pair of cards and reverse their positions before you place them on the pile. In other words, at each step you make an arbitrary choice—either put a single card on the pile or put down a pair after you have moved the top card below the other one. The purpose of this procedure is to destroy the ordering of the cards.

After you have gone through all thirteen cards, pick up the pile and repeat the procedure, deciding at random whether to deal one card or a reversed pair.

After this repeat dealing, how are the spades arranged?

Answer on page 81.

Insect, Animal, Bird

Think of a foreign country with a name that begins with A. Without taking a long time to think, write down:

1. The name of an insect that begins with the last letter of the country you thought of.

2. A wild animal with a name that starts with the last letter of the insect.

3. A bird that begins with the last letter of the animal.

Answers on page 84.

The Six Glasses

Arrange six drinking glasses in a row. Assume they are numbered 1, 2, 3, 4, 5, 6, from the left. Drop a penny into glass 1. Now, you must move the penny as you spell the professor's name.

A move consists of pouring the penny from one glass to the *nearest* glass on either side.

Spell PROFESSOR by making a move for each letter. When you finish, take away glass 1.

Now spell PICANUMBA. Take away glass 2.

Spell your last name twice. Take away glass 6.

Make one final move.

In what glass is the penny?

Answer on page 87.

End of a Chain

Think of any three-digit number with no two of its digits alike. Write the digits in ascending and descending order. Subtract the smaller number from the larger to get a second number. For example, if you thought of 614 you would subtract 146 from 641.

Arrange the new number's digits in ascending and descending order. Subtract the smaller from the larger to get a third number.

Keep doing this until you reach a number that keeps repeating itself.

What is this number that ends the chain?

Answer on page 82.

A Yardstick Prediction

Using tape, fasten two quarters, one on top of the other, at one end of a yardstick so they cover the inch from 35 to 36. Rest the yardstick on top of your hands as shown.

Bring your hands together slowly, moving each hand at any speed you like. When your palms touch you will be surprised to find that the yardstick remains balanced on your fingers.

What is the number on the yardstick nearest the spot where your palms touch?

Answer on page 90.

In Praise of Blue

Barbara's eyes are a beautiful blue.

On a bluebell, a blue butterfly.

I seldom am blue in December.

Though frequently blue in July.

A blue cheese is tasty on salads.

Blue berries are great in a pie.

But the most wonderful blue of all

Is the blue of a cloudless sky.

Roll a die. The number that comes up indicates a line in the above poem. Now look at the bottom face of the die. This tells you how to count to a word in the selected line.

What word do you reach?

Answer on page 83.

Odd or Even?

Put ten cards face down on the table, spread apart in any pattern you like. Now turn over cards as follows:

Reverse any single card, then reverse any pair of cards, then any three cards, and so on until you reverse all ten cards.

Count the number of face-up cards. Is it odd or even?

Answer on page 85.

A Row of Nine

From a deck, remove nine cards with values of ace (one) through nine. Arrange them in a row, face down and in counting order, starting with the ace on the left.

Select a card at either end of the row, and remove it from the row. Turn it face up.

Again, choose either end of the row. Slide the card from the row and turn it over.

Repeat this a third time, again picking a card from either end at random.

Add the values of the three cards randomly selected and removed. Divide the sum by 6. Call the result "n."

Look at the row's "n"th card. What value does it have?

Here's a funny story for you. Ms. Ames was startled to read, in a student's essay, that a neighbor, Mr. Jones, "always walks naked down the street." As quickly as she could, she phoned the student's parents. They confirmed that it was true...then they all laughed! How come?

Answers on page 86.

Nine-Card Spell

Remove nine cards from the deck. Shuffle them, then hold them face down in your left hand. Reverse the third card from the top of the packet.

Spell the name of the reversed card as follows. Let's assume it was the queen of hearts.

Spell Q-U-E-E-N by dealing five cards to the table, one card for each letter. Place the remaining cards on top of the five just dealt.

Pick up the packet. Spell O-F by dealing two cards to the table. Again, put the remaining cards on top of those just dealt.

Now spell H-E-A-R-T-S. Put the cards in your hand on top of the tabled pile.

Follow this procedure, using the name of the card you have reversed. Note that the number of letters in the name can vary from 10 (for example, the ace of clubs) to 15 (for example, the eight of diamonds).

After spelling the name of the reversed card, how far down is it from the top of the packet?

Answer on page 85.

Lincoln Up or Down?

Toss a five dollar bill into the air and let it flutter to the floor. After the bill lands, will the top of the bill show Lincoln's picture?

Answer on page 84.

A Royal Finish

Arrange 26 cards so that face down, from top to bottom, the packet consists of the ace through king of hearts, in serial order, followed by the ace through king of spades, also in serial order.

As you deal the cards face down, stop at any of the hearts and turn it face up. You may do this with the ace or king or any heart in between.

Count the number of letters in the name of the card's value. For example, ace is 3, the two is 3, the three is 5, and so on, call this number "k", deal "k" more cards, then turn the "k"th card face up. Again count the letters in the name of the card's value, and deal that number of cards, turning face up the card at the end of the count. Continue dealing and counting in this way, reversing a card at the end of each count, until you can't go any further.

What is the last card you turn face up?

Answer on page 87.

77

Twinkle, Twinkle

Believe it or not, you are featured in this familiar poem:

> Twinkle, twinkle, little star,
> How I wonder what you are
> Up above the world so high,
> Like a diamond in the sky.
> Twinkle, twinkle, little star,
> How I wonder what you are.

Select any word in the poem's first two lines. Spell the word by tapping the words ahead in the manner described in this book's first test (page 5). Keep going until your spelling chain can't continue any farther.

On what word does the count end?

Answer on page 89.

The Professor Predicts

Here are Professor Picanumba's predictions: the answers that he foresaw or said that you would likely give in doing these tests. A marvelous gift to have, isn't it!

An ABCABC Number

The number on display is the three-digit number you first thought of!

Another Calculator Surprise

The surprise is that the digits 1 through 9 are now in serial order starting with 1.

To make the tossed ball come back, toss it straight up in the air.

Another Calculator Test

You stopped your count on the heart.

Around the Circle

The count ends on the spiral.

Around the Solar System

If you moved correctly, the dime is on Pluto.

Around the Square

Your count ended on the letter D.

At the Apex

The triangle's top digit is 4.

Beast, City, Vegetable

Professor Picanumba guesses that the words are lion, Paris, and carrot.

A Calculator Test

The calculator displays 5.5.

Cards that Shake Dice

The sum of all the dice "throws" is 84.

Catch the Bill

You can't catch the bill before it drops.

Count the Clips

There are six paper clips left in the box.

A Curious Count

The number of undealt cards is 8.

The Curious Q

The last symbol you tapped is the star.

Deal and Switch

The thirteen spades are back in their original order, ace to king, with the ace on top.

A Domino Chain

The spots at the end of the domino chain will be 2 and 5.

Drop the Coin

Impossible, says Professor Picanumba.

An 8-Card Test

The four cards will have a sum of 38.

End of a Chain

The number that ends the chain is 495.

The Exact Word

"The exact word." Sorry about that!

Face-Up Cards

The difference is zero. The number of face-up cards in one pile will exactly equal the number of face-up cards in the other pile!

Five Coins

The folder is on the nickel.

Five in a Row

Professor Picanumba is not always right on this one, but he thinks you selected the four of hearts.

Fold and Trim

The face-up numbers will have the sum of 68.

A Four-Dice Test

The sum of the top faces of the four dice is 14.

Four File Cards

The product of the numbers on the file cards is 5,860,920.

Four Kings

The four cards on top of each pile are the four kings.

Four Knights

The four colors are each white.

Four Queens

The four cards are the four queens!

Funny Fractions

The difference is zero.

A Geometry Test

Professor Picanumba isn't sure, but he suspects you either put a circle inside a triangle, or a triangle inside a circle.

The GRY Test

The word you thought of was either "hungry" or "angry."

You were born within four days of Wednesday, and the cowboy's horse was named Friday.

Heads or Tails?

There will be more heads than tails.

In Praise of Blue

The word is "blue."

In Praise of Red

The word is "red."

Insect, Animal, Bird

Professor Picanumba guesses that you wrote ant, tiger, and robin.

A Letter in Washington

The letter in Washington is O. Professor Picanumba isn't positive he got this right, but he is almost certain he did.

Lincoln Up or Down?

The answer is yes. Professor Picanumba apologizes for this "swindle" because no matter which way the bill falls, he can't lose. On the back of the five dollar bill there is another picture of Lincoln. It shows him seated in front of the Lincoln Memorial in Washington, D.C.

The Magic of 8

The final digit is 8.

The Missing 8

The digit you selected is repeated in the display nine times. Professor Picanumba adds: Try dividing any digit except 0 by 9.

Monkey Business

You'd have six bananas left. (It's important to read tests carefully.)

A Mysterious Matrix

The sum of the six circled numbers is 111.

Nation, Animals, Fruit

The five words are Denmark, elephant, gray, kangaroo, and orange.

As for your shoes, you got 'em on your feet!

Nine-Card Spell

The reversed card is fifth from the top.

Number, Flower, Color

Professor Picanumba isn't positive, but his best guesses are 37, rose, and blue.

Number Names

The number that ends the chain is 4.

Odd or Even?

The number of face-up cards is odd.

One, Two, Three

The word is "the."

Pairing Cards

The difference is 4. There will be four more cards in the face-down pile than there are cards in the face-up pile.

A Peculiar Series

Check the last two numbers of the year that this book was published. It's on page 2, the copyright page which comes right after the title page, after the symbol ©.

The Red and the Black

The difference between the black and the red cards is 4.

The product of all ten digits is zero.

A Remarkable Number

The six-digit number is 124578.

Reverse, Subtract, Add

The word is "star."

The Rotated Die

The sum is odd.

A Rotating Matrix

The count ended on a cross.

Rotating Spoon

Professor Picanumba says that no matter how hard you try, when you catch the spoon its bowl will be right side up. He says he doesn't know why this is always the case.

The Rotating Tubes

The yardstick travels to one side until it falls off the tubes.

A Row of Nine

The row's "n"th card is four.

Mr. Jones was walking his dog Naked, a perfectly capital fine thing to do. (Remember to capitalize proper nouns.)

A Royal Finish

The card at the end of your counting chain is the king of spades.

The Six Glasses

The penny is in the middle glass of the three remaining glasses.

The Stubborn Rubber Band

Professor Picanumba bets you won't be able to do it.

The answer to the riddle is not 50, but 200. Ten divided by 1/2 is 20.

A Surprising Fraction

The final fraction is 1/3.

A Surprising Sum

The total of the four random numbers is 22,222.

Test of Finger Strength

Professor Picanumba says you can't do it.

The correct way to pronounce the capital of Kentucky is Frankfort.

A Test with 66

The result is 34.

There was no card-playing on the Ark because Noah sat on the deck.

A Test with Two Dice
The sum of the four products is 49.

A Test with Your Age
The number on display is 238.

Think-a-Digit
The number on display is 37.

Think-a-Letter
The letter will be the letter you first thought of.

A 3 by 4 Test
The final digit is 3.

A Three-Dice Stack
The sum of the five hidden faces is 20.

Three Heaps
The number of clips in the center heap is 10.

Three Surprises
In each case the result is your age repeated three times.

Topsy Turvy Fun
The upside-down words are HELLO, GOSH, HO-HO-HO, and BOISE.

A Trick With Three Dice

The result is 21.

Try This on a Dollar Bill

The final digit is 2.

Turn Two and Cut

There are five face-up cards in the row.

Twinkle, Twinkle

The count ends on "you."

A Two-Dice Test

The final sum is 21.

246,913,578

The number is 123456789.

An Unexpected Number

You get pi (the circumference of a circle with a diameter of 1) correct to eleven decimal places except for the ninth decimal, which should be 3 instead of 2.

What's on the Paper?

You are on the paper.

To see through walls, look through a window.

What's the Word?

The word you spell is CAGE.

Where's the Ace?

The ace of spades will be the ninth card from the top.

Where's the Dime?

The dime is on square K.

Whisk the Dime

The dime refuses to be brushed off your palm.

The riddle's answer is that the barber would make ten times as much money.

Wonderland Spell

The word is "sister."

A Yardstick Prediction

Your palms come together at the 21 mark.

Epilogue

By now, I'm sure you realize that Professor Picanumba is an imaginary character having no more psychic powers than you or I do. All the tests in this book have pre-determined outcomes that are either absolutely certain or have a high probability of being correct.

The tests make excellent "magic" tricks to show friends. Depending on the test, you can present them in different ways. One way is to have someone go through the steps of a test while your back is turned, so you can't possibly see what he or she is doing—such as entering numbers in a calculator. With your back still turned, rub your forehead while you make believe you are concentrating on the "vibes," then announce the test's final result as if you obtained it by reading your friend's mind.

The other way to present a trick is by pretending you have the wondrous powers of precognition—that is, an ability to foresee or know the future. Write your prediction on a sheet of paper and place it face down on the table. At the end of the exercise, have your friend turn over the sheet, and read what you have written. He or she will be astounded to see that you have correctly predicted the results of the test.

If you are intrigued and want to try figuring out why one or more of these tests work, be my guest. You are sure to learn a great deal about mathematics by doing so. If a few should prove especially puzzling to you, perhaps your math teacher (if you are a student) will consider making deciphering them a fun class exercise, or someone knowledgeable about math can explain the workings of some of these seemingly magical tests.

You must admit, there is something spooky and beautiful about the laws of mathematics!

About the Author
Martin Gardner

World-famous as the puzzlemaster who wrote the "Mathematical Games" column of *Scientific American* magazine for 25 years, Martin Gardner has also written close to 70 books, on such subjects as science (including a book that *Time* magazine called "by far the most lucid explanation of Einstein's theories"), mathematics, philosophy, religion, poetry, literary criticism (including *The Annotated Alice*, a classic examination of *Alice in Wonderland* that is still selling large numbers of copies now, 40 years after it was first published) and, of course, puzzles (out of 29 puzzle books for adults and children, only one is out of print!).

The son of an Oklahoma wildcat oil prospector, Gardner attended the University of Chicago, where he received a degree in philosophy. After graduation he worked on the *Tulsa* (Oklahoma) *Tribune*. He sold his first story to *Esquire*, published articles on logic and math in specialist magazines and became a contributing editor to *Humpty Dumpty's Magazine* before starting his legendary column.

Martin Gardner has had a lifelong passion for conjuring, and many of his original magic tricks have become classics among magicians.

Dubbed "The Magician of Math" by *Newsweek*, Martin Gardner, now retired, makes his home in North Carolina, where he continues to amaze his fans with more and more books, articles and ideas.

Index

Page key: test, *prediction (solution)*.